How to Write
30 Books
In
30 Days

Learn the secrets to producing amazing
quality content at blinding speed!

About the author

Danial Barron Howe is the author of over 350 books (under multiple pen names) ranging from business and online income to health and wellness. He is the founder of six multinational businesses including **2ndEmpireMedia**, the publisher of this book and **TheMinuteMarketer.Com** , a rapidly growing community catering to the ongoing education of information marketers.

Dan has been involved in the information marketing business ever since he wrote his first book, *POWER PROFITS!* Nearly a decade and a half ago. Since that time he has gone on to sell over 750,000 books in both printed and electronic form as well as numerous audio, video and other hybrid forms of informational products.

In addition to his role as an informational product producer, he holds several degrees including a Masters in mechanical engineering and design as well as degrees in psychology and biomechanics. He is a lifelong tinkerer artist and visionary innovator with a passion for improving efficiencies of systems such as those found within this book.

Forward

Can you really produce 30 quality books in only 30 days?
Believe it or not, the answer is *"yes"*! A mere 29 days ago I sat down at my computer with the objective of pulling off what some would consider a *minor miracle*, and today I will complete book number 30 of my marathon campaign - appropriately enough titled *"How to write 30 books in 30 days!"*

For me, this seemingly incredible feat wasn't really that difficult at all. Over the years I have developed *a system* for creating book after book. By using my special system I'm able to insert segments of original content into one of the many pre-existing templates I've developed for many different genres.

Why should you listen to me?
I am a chronic workaholic, multi track serial entrepreneur who never seems to sit still for very long or stay focused on any one thing for any extended period of time. And on top of it all, I'm dyslexic too! Despite this, I still managed to author over 350 books in under 24 months without the use of subcontractors or virtual assistants! If I can achieve this level of output despite my hectic schedule, I'm quite confident you can do the same – *or even better!*

I can't write your books for you, nor can I market them for you. What I *will do* is teach you how to develop a group of ideas and get them all into book form incredibly quickly. My techniques above all else are what will separate you from those that never seem to get anything finished or put out for public consumption, despite otherwise having very marketable ideas.

What you can expect from this book.
I created this book as a personal challenge to myself. I have often claimed that it was possible to write *a book a day* if you really set your mind to it. Despite what many people would consider "*a dyslexic disadvantage*", I love to write! I once heard someone say that "*you don't know what you know until you teach it to someone else!*"

Once I finally do set aside the time to write I'm often surprised by the endless number of amazing ideas that seem to pour out of me when I *get in the zone* and am able to sit down, focus and put together my latest book or course. If you're having a hard time getting started just remember: simply taking action creates *more action*.

I'm sure you have something to teach the world as well. The knowledge you have built up over the years is in there, rattling around in your head, just waiting to come out. Forget the notion that you need to be the ultimate authority on any subject to write about it. Or that you need an official stamp of approval put on you by some four-year college. What matters is letting the world hear your unique perspective.

I promise you this: The system I will teach you here in this book will unlock a wellspring of ideas and a geyser of creativity! By the time you finish this book *you will have a workable plan for creating no less than one book every single day* if you choose to.

I am a full-time information marketer and author.
Let me be clear upfront; I am not going to fill your head full of theoretical nonsense or recycled gibberish that I've pulled from various places all over the Internet. *I am a full time professional information marketer and 350+ title book author.* I'm in the trenches each day earning a living by the skills that I've acquired over a decade and a half of actual use. I have to, this is how I feed myself and my family! If you are looking for straightforward, candid advice on what works then follow me, I will get you where you want to go!

… And now for a shameless marketing plug:
Although the information in this book will take you a long, long way in the understanding of setting up your own mini publishing empire, the tips found here are only a few of the many tools available to you and you should always be on the lookout for more. You wouldn't expect to build a house using just one hammer would you?

When you're ready to take your book marketing to the next level, visit me at my site. I've put together a *virtual toolbox* of resources for you to use in your promotional efforts.

www.TheMinuteMarketer.Com

Index

Preface

What does it takes to make a living as an author?
When you look at the statistics for failed business
startups in general, the prospects are pretty dismal.
Why do so many fail? Generally the answer falls into
three categories:

1. They are inadequately funded
2. The owners lack an essential skill or knowledge
   (or at the very least a workable plan)
3. But the biggest ones are *loss of motivation or
   focus*… These are quite common for most
   would-be authors.

The good news is that by using my system all of these
common stumbling blocks can be easily avoided. In
addition, I will show you the best of everything I know
about how to set yourself up for success right here
within the chapters of this book.

British Prime Minister Winston Churchill, famously
addressed a graduating class. When asked to speak he
stood up, walked to the podium, quietly surveyed the
crowd in attendance and instead of delivering an
expectedly long winded speech, he simply announced
*"Never give up! Never give up! **Never, <u>ever</u> give up!***"
and with that he returned to his seat…. nuff said.

Building a sustainable business with eBooks is a numbers game.
It may come across as obvious to many of you, but understanding this fact is the key to success. The misunderstanding many beginning authors have is to expect to create *a single title* that will produce a flood of traffic and income year after year. Yes, it can happen but it's not very often. So that generally speaking, that type of thinking won't get you very far.

To be a successful you must have *many hooks (books) in the water* as possible at any given time. Amazon allows you to post an unlimited amount of unique publications and successful authors and sellers know how to take advantage of that fact. When it comes to e-books, *volume rules!* Some will make you a little bit of money, while others could make you a lot!

There is a clear case to be made for producing multiple books
The reality is that if you only put up a couple of books on Amazon (or any other e-book seller for that matter) and expect the traffic to beat a path to your door you're likely going to come away sorely disappointed. Amazon's kindle program is growing by leaps and bounds and its user base is currently in the multiple millions. However, there's only so much room on the top page to be a featured seller. If you're not coming up in the searches it's unlikely anyone will ever know you exist. This presents a problem; *how will the buyers find you?* The answer rests solely on the actions that you take to actively promote your books on your own.

By creating multiple titles you can *cross-link* them together, thereby increasing the likelihood that your entire catalog of offerings will be exposed to all new readers who come across one of your books, even if it's only by random chance. I'll cover more about cross-linking your titles together later on in the book, but for now I want you to understand that when it comes to producing those multiple titles, the ones who are claiming the largest amount of search *engine real estate* are the ones who come away as the biggest winners.

Relax, everything you need to succeed is already at hand.
Promotion of any kind isn't rocket science. We'll go over some of the finer points of promotion as well. My philosophy defines promotion and has finding relevant groups of interested people and letting them know where to find you (or maybe just making your first introduction.). I'll show you how to do that in upcoming chapters

Let me assure you that you don't need a sparkling personality or outstanding speaking skills to promote your book. (Even when it comes time to make your promotional Youtube video) Heck, you don't honestly need the looks of a Hollywood actor and you really don't even need a great education. I've seen several successful examples of this theory all over Amazon! All you need to do is a little one time work to develop a well laid out, organized presentation and know how to deliver it in the most effective manner.

What DO you need most to be successful?
Volume! As I said before, success with Amazon is a numbers game. The more you put yourself out there, the closer you come to greater and greater success as an

author and seller. Don't worry, you WILL get there, but I won't try to kid you and tell you that it doesn't take an investment of your time and effort up front to start things moving. But, just picture yourself sitting on a tropical beach while the rest of the world deposits automatic money into your account from sales you made on Amazon and others. People do a lot more difficult things all over this Earth every day for the sake of a "job".

*(No doubt you've heard this "dream scenario" many times before but I can tell you **this is my reality!** Kindle publishing has allowed me to move from America to an island paradise here in the Philippines. As I sit here dictating this book I'm on the back deck of my house overlooking the crashing waves of the China Sea. Rough life eh?*

What if I do something wrong or nobody buys my books?
Don't worry, you'll screw up and you'll probably get involved in many unproductive activities more than once that will make you will want to quit and lick your wounds. It's happened to the best of us.

Here's my best advice; *Get over yourself!* This is a learning process and nobody learns by succeeding all the time. If you picked the wrong topic (unlikely), designed a horrible book cover (happens quite often), or just lacked the confidence it takes to make a well presented promotional audio or video, learn from it! Make the appropriate adjustments and then move on. Never give up!

My secret:
Do you want to know a secret that very few beginning e-book authors recognize when faced with a situation like this? We live in the digital age. NOTHING ONLINE IS PERMANENT. Amazon doesn't put a limit on the amount of corrections you can make once you publish your work. Those corrections can be made with just a few keystrokes and the click of a mouse. If you don't like the way something looks after glancing at it a second or third time, fix it! New potential visitors will never know how bad things used to be.

Really, every time you develop a new book title you are beginning with a clean slate (especially if you publish your works under multiple pen names). Once you have learned the basics, then you'll have your own template to work from. The truth; is there is no reason to be embarrassed or worry about ruining your reputation. Unless you are a well-known celebrity most visitors to your sale page could care less who you are, as long as what you're providing is of sufficient value to them.

The biggest mistake you can make.
The truth is; not every book on Amazon is worth a damn. No matter how amazing you may believe your offer is, or how snazzy the promotional materials or book cover looks. It doesn't even matter how slick your description is. Bottom line: Amazon buyers vote with their wallets. If you're not making sales the problem is something you're doing is not resonating with buyers and if you fail to address this fact you will never hit the big time.

Often times new authors with no formal promotional skills jump headlong into book ideas that they *think* the public would be interested in, never doing even the least little bit of research to find out if there *actually even is* a market. My advice here is simple: proceed intelligently. If you're unsure the market size, test things out with a lower-priced $.99 book (you really have nothing to lose - it's always free to write and post your books) and see what kind of traffic comes of it before getting crazy and going all out with a larger size book.

The greatest system of the 21st century.
Throughout the course of my life I have been involved in many, many different enterprises. I have been a real estate investor, television producer, professional motorcycle manufacturer, and a whole host of other things. Each business came with its benefits and drawbacks however, few ever provided me the free time to actually enjoy my life the way marketing informational products has. The internet has truly revolutionized the way business can be done – *but if*

and only if you learn the rules first!

I can say without a doubt that developing informational products and eBooks and then marketing them through my various sales channels such as my websites, blogs, Youtube videos and yes, even fiverr as well has been an ongoing challenge and a thrill for me.

Sure, there was a learning curve with all of it, there always is. But, once I crossed that threshold into knowledge and proficiency I was able to enjoy a lifestyle that few will ever able to experience.

If you desire a life filled with more free time, the ability to apply your creativity in myriads of ways and a potentially far better rate of pay then you're currently earning, remember the words of Winston Churchill; *"Never give up! Never give up! Never, ever give up!"*

Ready? Then let's get started!

The tools of the trade

Besides a simple basic computer, you'll need a couple of other specialized items:

- **Dragon naturally speaking** voice to text transcription software.

- **Microsoft word** (or if you can't afford that, also get started with OpenOffice.org –a freeware equivalent)

- **Corel artistic software** (for the book cover design - if you're the hands-on type)

Dragon 101
The day I discovered ***Dragon naturally speaking*** software my productivity totally exploded! I speak at a very rapid fire pace to begin with but never formally learned to type. To make matters worse, my mind is always running multiple tracks. Needless to say typing is a chore for me.

With the Dragon software I'm able to "spit out" a stream of consciousness that isn't slowed down by hunting all over my keyboard for a missing letter or even remembering how to spell, it's all done for me automatically!

Why Microsoft word?
Don't get me wrong, I'm not "*Pro Microsoft*". In fact, I don't really care one way or another what word processing software you choose. They all work pretty

much the same in most cases. However, that does not necessarily mean they are compatible with the Dragon software, and that's why I choose Microsoft word.

I respect the idea that not everyone has discretionary income and you may not be able to initially afford to purchase word. With that being said, you can freely download a very usable alternative at OpenOffice.org. Just be aware that you may have to "tweak" some of the settings to get them to work fluidly with the Dragon software. I've used OpenOffice several times myself with mixed results. Often times I get things dialed in just the way I like and then they do a software update and then I have to fix things all over again!

I'm not an *Apple guy* so I'm sorry that I can't personally report on any compatibility issues with Dragon for your equivalent software, however, I have it on good authority that you should have no problems.

Corel design software.
If you're going to design your own e-book covers you're going to need a high quality design program that can do the job for you. Because your book cover represents the "face" of your product that people see when they are deciding to make a purchase, this is not the place to scrimp and use the free built-in tools that come with your computer. Listen to my advice here: Use professional graphic design software. The results you will get are far superior to anything you can do pull off using freebies.

My personal preference is Corel design because I believe it is simpler, and more intuitive than anything currently being offered by Adobe (i.e. Photoshop, illustrator, InDesign, etc.). Not to mention it costs a heck of a lot less too! You can create some amazing cover designs in about an hour without too much of a learning curve.

Researching A Winning Topic

You probably already have a pretty good idea what you want to write about or you may have already gotten started, and there's nothing wrong with that. However, when it comes to picking winning topics, the best way to proceed is to *do your research before you get started putting any words on the page* (or up on the screen).

In this chapter we'll discuss how to use free tools such as **Google's Ad Words tool** to seek out large groups of perspective buyers and you will learn how to craft the general flavor of your book to appeal to the largest number of readers in that target group.
Will

John knew "the secret".
When notorious robber John Dillinger was asked *why he robbed banks* his answer was very simple; *"Because that's where all the money is!"* he would answer. Hard to argue with that logic…

With regard to your efforts as a kindle writer, let me pose this question to you; *do you know how to find YOUR "BANK" of willing buyers?* John knew what he was after – and how to get it. *Do you?* Don't get me wrong, I'm not suggesting you bend the law in any way, I'm merely illustrating an attention to focus, preparation and execution.

Being successful at any endeavor requires being prepared for that success in advance. That requires planning coupled with intelligent research. And that's what I am going to teach you how to do.

Google ad words tool.
If you don't already have a Google account, get one
now. It's about impossible to do any amount of quality
keyword research (especially for free) without
involving one or more of Google's free utilities. Yes,
Bing has a free keyword research tool of their own as
well, but why mess around with *second fiddle?* Google
is the king when it comes to search engines and there's
strength in numbers.

Once you've gotten signed up for a free Google account
logon to **Adwords.Com** and locate the *tools* option at
the top of the screen and then select *keyword planner*
from the drop-down menu. And then select option one-
search for new keyword.

Why are we here?
If you did everything correctly you should be looking at a gray box that looks like the one below.

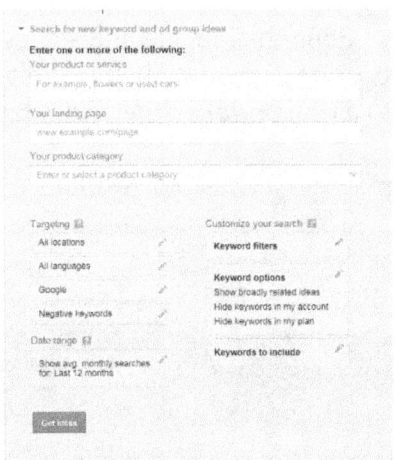

This box is where we will begin our search for *popular topics* to write books on. The best way to begin is pick something you're interested in and start there. Let's say for example you are interested in *competitive bicycling.*

Common sense should tell you there's only so many people that are interested in that topic so perhaps we should start with the broader search -say for example *cycling.* Enter that term in the top box and hit the *get ideas* button.

On the next screen you should see a jumble of data. Pay no mind to it *yet.* We still have some organizing to do before we're ready to make any sense of it.

Find and select the *keyword Ideas* tab located next to the ad group ideas tab and select it.

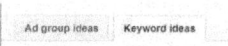

Once you have done this, locate and select the *average monthly searches* section and click at the top to get it reshuffled into a *descending order* from largest to smallest.
We are now ready to assess our results.

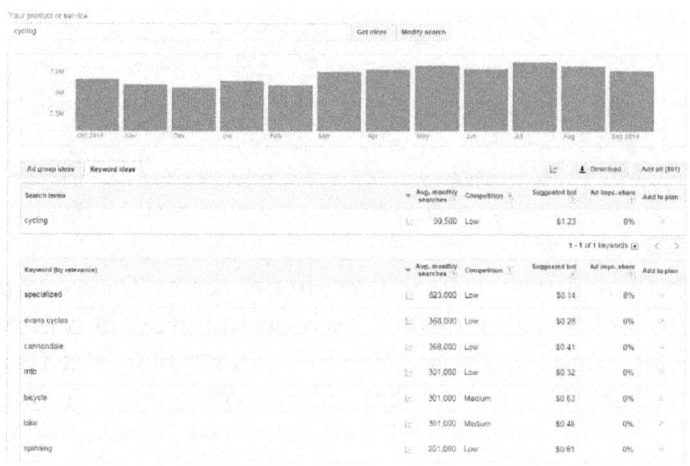

Taking a close look at the output, you notice our original search term is highlighted above all the others, showing a monthly count of 90,500 searches worldwide. Not too shabby, but we can do better. Looking further down the list you'll see other searches that Google deems *relevant* to your initial search term (sometimes Google takes a few *liberties* and misses the mark but generally speaking there pretty spot on)

Taking a look at the top three positions we see the word *specialized* getting a massive 823,000 searches a month! That's impressive, but nothing you can write a book about so let's keep looking.

Spot number two is *Williams Cycles* and Spot three belongs to *Cannondale*, a brand of high-end bike, with Google searches exceeding 350,000 a month!

While I don't know anything about Williams's cycles, I *do know* Cannondale has a pretty strong following. Armed with that little bit of personal knowledge, I feel like a book could be made related to Cannondale bicycles based upon the strong number of searches and I feel it would be a pretty easy seller provided you could gather enough content to create a compelling book.

Looking a little further down our list we find keywords like *bicycle (301,000 monthly searches), bike (also with 301,000) and spinning* (at 201,000).* The monthly search traffic on all three indicates a strong interest and therefore all three of these would make great basic topics for eBooks.

*If you not familiar with spinning it's a form of stationary bicycle exercise.

How low should you go?
When searching for keywords I'm often asked by readers *what I consider to be the lowest acceptable monthly search number for a niche topic.* That's a tough question to answer because sometimes the pools of buyers just aren't that big to begin with however, I tend to shy away from keywords with anything less

than 50,000 to 60,000 monthly searches.

There's enough topics to write about in this world that there is no sense in starving yourself to death because you're interested in a topic or diving into a shallow pool of buyers with little chance of being rewarded for the time spent.

What do I do now?
This brief *keyword research run through* is only meant to be just a primer, however, if you repeat the process I just showed you again and again, you will come up with *literally thousands* of outstanding topics to write books on and you'll know for a fact that there is a willing public ready to buy, after all, they are searching those very topics! All you need to do is round up 30 or so of those high traffic key words, center a book idea around each them and get to writing!
Yes, It really is just that easy!

Many *Kindle gurus* will tell you that you have to search on Amazon and in hundreds of different places, or by some special program to unlock the secrets of what customers want. To this I say *"Bull!"* If you spend your time looking for keywords with big search numbers and you **center your books topics and marketing on those search terms** you are going to move some books… *lots* and lots of books! The search engine results don't lie.

The Boilerplate Concept

In this chapter we will cover the idea of assembling books using a *pre-formatted template* that will save you time and serve as a backbone for each new book you create.

Boilerplate
This term refers to the commonly used pre-existing language that must be a part of every legal document. Most legal professionals keep an entire catalog full of examples of boilerplate documents on hand for just about any occasion such as wills, purchase agreements, eviction notices, petitions and more.

I first became acquainted with the concept of boilerplate documents back in my real estate days. Often times I would find myself in need of legal services to prepare documents for purchases and sales. Pressed for time one evening on a house closing, In a moment of unusual candor my attorney told me *"I'll just pull a standard form out of my drawer and change the relevant information"*.

"Wait a minute!" I thought to myself. *"Did he say he was going to pull a **premade form** out of his desk, change a few words and then charge me $350?"* Yep, he did! In fact, a great majority of the legal profession works this way.* Most legal forms are *preprinted and standardized*, requiring only the addition of specific information to make them a ***unique document***.

*Think about this next time you find yourself in need of an expensive "hard-working" attorney!

Building your very own "boilerplate book".
When considering how to most efficiently create our
next book, we can draw some great lessons from the
above example. Every book contains within it many
elements that are repeated every time we create a new
project (opening credits, publisher information, indexes,
chapter headers and such)–that's *our* boilerplate!

By devising our own *ready to go* document containing
all the commonly reused elements found in a typical
book in our pre-filled out form, we'll have a template to
work with that simply requires us to insert the relevant
information to create a completely unique work!*

*If you want to understand how powerful this concept can be consider
this; I'm currently using a template to write this very book. When I started
off I already had 3500+ words prefilled out! If your goal is to write a
10,000 to 15,000 word book that can shave some *serious* time off of your
writing!

Book Anatomy 101

This chapter will discuss the basic layout and structure you will need to have in place to create you book templates. We'll cover how to catalog different templates and how to modify them for additional uses.

Let's take a look at the structure of a typical book. Most every *commercially published* book has within it certain common elements that can be universally found in most books (and are generally expected to be there by readers as well).
These elements include:

- Book title page
- ISBN and publishing information page
- A dedication page
- Possibly a legal disclaimer page
- A preface
- Table of contents
- A Forward by the author
- *Possible supporting photos, charts or graphics throughout the book
- Author notes
- Bibliography
- …and an Index

Knowing this, we can begin to envision the outline of a document that will allow us to have *a ready to go template* to build multiple books from.

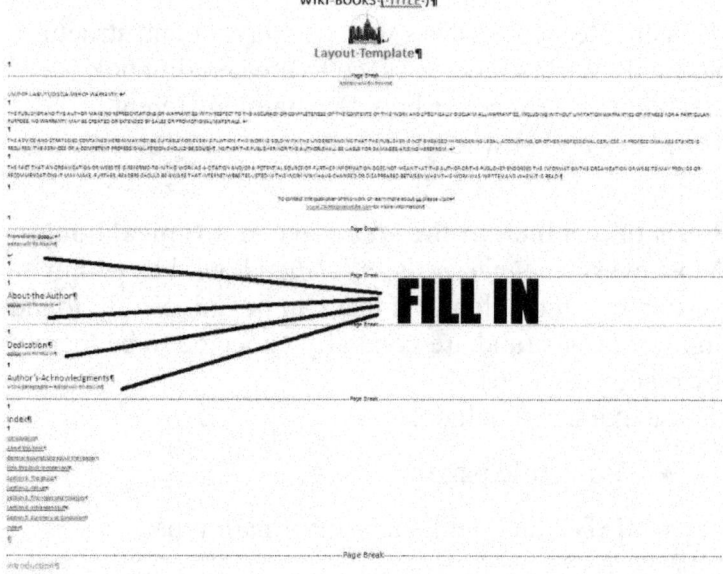

As you can see from the illustration above, when we remove the original text from between these standard boilerplate components we are left with *"holes"* in our document. These holes are where we will fill in the original new content each time we create a book.

Read 3 Books

Marketing guru Dan Kennedy is fond of saying that *you only need to read three books on any given subject to be more of an expert on that topic than 99% of the public*. This is actually pretty straightforward advice- and a big time saver when it comes to research as well!

Assuming you've done your keyword research to look for a popular topic (as outlined in an earlier chapter), you could follow Dan's advice and simply consume three Kindle e-books in a matter of a few of hours. After taking notes on the common highlights of each, you would have the basic outline of your own unique book roughed out in no time flat!

Breaking big tasks into little efforts.
If you want to see how easy all this really is, let's look at it this way; assume you read three books. Let's further assume that the book you plan to write is 9,000 words, we already know that once we fill in our *formatting* and our *boilerplate* we've chewed up potentially 2000 words of our total goal. That leaves roughly 7000 words to get up on screen.

If we divide those 7000 remaining words by each of our three books that leaves us 2333 words per book to summarize… When you look at it that way, it's not really that difficult is it?

Fire Up Your Dragon

In this chapter will go over a few of the key set up steps of the Dragon transcription software and discuss how to best use it with the template system covered in this book.

The essence of my entire speed writing technique centers on the use of **Nuance's Dragon Naturally Speaking** *Voice to text transcription software*. If you choose to go *old school* and hack away at your keyboard instead of following my lead with this amazing program, go ahead and jump to the next chapter. As for the rest of you, let's get things set up and ready to roll.

Out of the box Dragon comes with an install Cd on all levels and if you choose more advanced versions they come with headphones as part of the package. There really is no difference in which package you get. The included software is basically all the same.

My advice here is if you have a pair headphones with a built-in mic that you prefer already, use them. I'm not a huge fan of the headphones that come with the software anyway. They seem a little flimsy to me and personally I like to use my Logitech wireless headphones anyway. That way I'm not tied to my desk and I can wonder around the house and dictate and the same time.

Getting to know you.
Once you've installed your Dragon software you will need to go through a short *training session* with it to dial in your microphone and allow it to understand how

you pronounce words and build sentence structure.

The folks at Nuance understand there's no such thing as one-size-fits-all software so when setting up your program it will not only what region of the country you come from just for southern dialects, but it will also ask you to input your age range (apparently the way we speak changes as we age- ha! who knew!?)

Lastly, you have the option of allowing Dragon to review old emails and documents you've prepared that are stored on your hard drive in order to discover the way you form sentences and what words you choose to express yourself. While some people might have issues with allowing software to go through their personal documents, you needn't worry. This is strictly an internal calibration procedure and can be done with the Internet connection turned off if you choose. It is however optional so you can pass on this part if you wish.

The longer you use Dragon the "smarter" it gets and the more *dialed in* to your speaking style it becomes. Remember: when shutting off your computer or turning off the program, always be sure to exit and let it completely go through its closing procedure so that it can save all that it's learned from the current session about your individual speech patterns for use in future sessions.

How I use Dragon to crank out a book a day.

As with anything, practice makes perfect and overtime you will develop your own style of writing using the software. For now though follow my lead so you can buzz through content creation for your books as rapidly as possible.

At this point in time you should have your template filled out with all your boilerplate items filled in (title, index header ideas for each chapter from your notes etc.). If you are using a mouse with scroll wheel roll the screen up to your first open *hole* in your template, turn on your Dragon software, place your cursor at the start of the paragraph and begin speaking your ideas onto the screen! It's thrilling to watch your words come to life isn't it?!

Once you've filled up that first section of your template with enough ideas then move on to the next one and the next one after that. Hemingway once said *"all first drafts are shit"*. At this point we're just *writing for the trash can* so don't be too judgmental, just get it out there and onto the screen.

Once you've reached the bottom of your template and filled in all the holes in your template then congratulate yourself. You now have your very own first draft!

If you're using Microsoft word take a look at the lower left corner of your screen and see what your page and word count currently is at. If you're publishing to

Amazon (and most others too) and want to sell your book in the $2.99 to $5.99 price range you should have roughly 10,000 to 15,000 words and about 65 to 80 pages when all is said and done (I'm working with the assumption that you're doing *nonfiction* as this is the going rate and expected size at this current moment).

If you're light on that count at this point you likely still have some refining and additions to make to your manuscript anyway. So go back up and place your cursor at any point in your template that needs doctoring up and speak a little more text into the paragraphs of your choice. This is the essence of how it's done;

Point-Click-Talk!

Establishing A "Sales Worthy" Page Count

Here's a question for you: Which book is larger by volume?

Book 1 with a page count of 1
Or
Book 2 with a page count of 500

The answer seems pretty straight forward at first blush doesn't it? But in the world of eBooks (*and kindle most specifically*) the answer isn't always so clear. Here's why…

When putting together your book on screen* you are not bound by the physical limitations of a *paper page*. You can write and write until your fingers go numb from all that typing and still never hit the limitations of your "page". While this may seem to be a blessing, it can actually work against you when it comes time to sell your book for top dollar.

Amazon gives its buyers very limited information concerning a books content beyond a cover picture, some past buyer feedback (if any), a price and what you tell the potential buyer in your books description. However, one additional bit of information Amazon *does give* is *number of pages,* and it can have a profound effect on your buyer's attitude towards what he or she perceives to be "*a value*".
Take a moment and see things from your buyer's perspective; would you be inclined to pay good money for a book if you thought it only had *one page*?

Proceeding with this understanding, clearly it would be in our best interest to upload a book that is correctly formatted with the highest possible page count.

Setting hard page breaks.
If you're new to word processing, you may be tempted to believe that simply hitting the *return* button a few times will have the "separating effect" you're looking for. You would be *incorrect* in that assumption.

Creating separate pages is done using the *page break* function. *In Microsoft word this is accomplished by holding down Ctrl while at the same time pressing return.* Once you've done this, you should see a line extending all the way across the screen breaking up your long column of text and moving everything below where your cursor was downward… Congratulations, you just created a page!

The subject of laying out e-books correctly is a subject unto itself. If you'd like a little more information on doing so a couple of good books I would suggest on this topic are:

How to write a book and sell it on amazon

The Book Marketing BIBLE

The Create Space And Kindle Self-Publishing Matrix

*I use Microsoft Word but pretty much all word processors work about the same.

Should You Bulk Up
With Photos?

Books are a *visual medium*. Whenever possible you should consider breaking up huge blocks of text not only by inserting page breaks as discussed in the last chapter, but also by inserting a related chart, picture or graphic of some sort. Here too however, eBooks differ greatly from their printed cousins and so some precautions must be taken and we'll discuss those here in a moment.

As you may well have discovered by now, resizing your kindle screen does not have the same effect on graphic scaling as it does on text and in some cases it has none at all. Authors wishing to clearly illustrate a point are not doing their readers much of a service by expecting them to make out the details of a photo that at times can be no larger than a postage stamp!*

Remember: The largest growing group of readers are using their smart phones. Tiny pictures on a 3.5 inch screen are NOT going to cut it!

Ask yourself; *"Is this picture really necessary?"*
It may strike you as a good idea to load up your new book full of high quality photos and illustrations but, if you go overboard with the pics you may be in for a surprise when it comes time to collect your royalties. Amazon charges its authors a ***delivery fee***, typically about .06 to .09 per downloaded book, provided you are selling a 10,000 to 15,000 word book with no illustrations in it. That figure can grow at a monumental pace (not to mention make for a horrible formatting nightmare) if you stuff hundreds of pictures into your

book. Best to take a moderate approach and really evaluate the need to include anything more than 5 to 6 well placed pics or charts at the most.

Minimize file size by reducing resolution

One way to "hack" the process and save a few bucks on delivery fees is to reduce your file size. Microsoft word users can do this by installing the graphic in the proper place by choosing [*Insert*] from the upper file menu and then [*Pictures*]. Once your picture is displayed on screen you may choose to center or resize it (smaller is better!). Under the FILE option choose [*Compress Pictures*] and choose [*Web Pictures*] from the pop up dialogue box. This will knock down the file size to 96 dpi or somewhere around there. You'll now likely notice a fuzzier appearance to your picture – this is normal and something that you just have to live with if you choose to go this route.

*This too can be a tradeoff however because with reduced resolution and file size comes diminished readability. So when considering this tip its best not do it when your file includes text.

An alternate way

Rather than creating a bulky eBook that costs you any unnecessary amazon transfer fees whatsoever, why not link to photos on your server or one of the many free photo sharing sights available all over the web instead? Besides the obvious cost savings from having a smaller book size, you will be able to display a larger, clearer picture to your reader by hosting the unrestricted photo elsewhere.

Share links with URL Shortners

Url shortners are programs that condense long web addresses down into shorter, more compacted bite sized pieces. Affiliate marketers have used them for years to cloak their affiliate links. Two of the most popular are *Bit.ly* and *Goog.gl*. Before you run off to check them out I want to give you a bit of advice on using these leading companies…*DON'T!*

Over the last few years (thanks largely to shady affiliate marketers) shortened urls have earned a dubious reputation. The net using public has grown leery of clicking on links they don't recognize (often resulting in viral downloads, erased back tracks or endless pop up assaults) most of these offenders used Bit.ly (many still do). To make matters worse, many large sites are beginning to reject Bit.ly links based on their sorted past. With that being said, why associate yourself with that negative experience in your buyers mind?

Goo.gl is another big player in the url shortening arena. Owned by Search engine goliath Google, goo.gl would seem to be a safe and logical choice for chopping down those unwieldy links…again, I say *"pass!"* I'm an affiliate marketer as well as an author and I have had many occasions to use goog.gl. Early on I was quite pleased. Everything was all in one place and I could easily access it under the same username and password I use for Gmail.

With time however, I begin to notice traffic to my affiliate sites was dropping at an alarming pace- right along with my income! As it turns out, google had been "flagging" the sites (not my links- but the actual affiliates) and effectively *"switching off"* any connection to those affiliates through my shortened url!* Google = Judge, jury....*and executioner!*

*I'm not **Anti-Google** but I really find many of their practices to be rather over the top. Besides, I think turning over too much of your business' future to such a large 3rd party company is just asking for trouble anyway. More than one little guy has already been crushed by recent search engine algorithm changes. Many we're flat out told that their sites were removed from the SERPs altogether!*

A new player enters the fray.
Recently I've discovered **Bit.Do** to put it mildly; *I'm a fan!* The Bit.Do user interface is clean and simple as expected however, where it really shines is the back end stats and the way you can easily access them.

Here's an example:

My original affiliate link to amazon would look like this:
http://www.amazon.com/gp/product/B00O2UP90A/ref =as_li_tl?ie=UTF8&camp=1789&creative=390957&c reativeASIN=B00O2UP90A&linkCode=as2&tag=wha mtrade-20&linkId=NR4QSJZSLJCKOA3T

That's a bit much to take in, and frankly impossible for a reader to remember, let alone retype if need be.

Using Bit.Do We can enter the above code and even pick a custom name too! *http://bit.do/30in30 Tah-DAH!*

...But wait, there's more!
Want to know how many people are hitting your new special custom link? That's easy to do by simply putting a " - " at the end of your new shortened url.

Like so: *http://bit.do/30in30-*

Click the example link above and you'll see tons of useful marketing information such as:

- *How many total page views you've have had*

- *How many desk tops vs mobile platforms are accessing your site.*

- *Referring sites*

- *Referring pages*

- *You can output it all in a spreadsheet*

- *You'll even get a custom QR code to use wherever you choose!*

This stuff is pure SEO & marketing gold!

In short; Bit.Do Does not participate in "traffic engineering" the way that google does and has not suffered the bad press of Bit.ly

Promote Your Work

Social media has its fair share of hype so I'll spare you the obvious suggestion to use it here because I'm sure you've read it all before. I'm not down on social media, not by a long shot. I just don't like to work that hard! If you're wanting a more passive way to promote your new books and totally slick way to grab top rankings on Google without learning SEO at the same time, Make mini videos and post them on Youtube.

Every marketer should have a **Youtube** channel. You should too! With *zero barrier to entry* why wouldn't you want a free opportunity to be listed with the world's first and second largest search engines?

Besides being able to post an unlimited number of promotional videos, When setting up your channel you also get an opportunity to link potential buyers back to your amazon books sale page or author page (assuming you have more than one book for sale....*and you should!*)

If you want to learn how to rapidly crank out several *mini promotional videos* for each of your books (and have the added advantage of gaining top search engine ranking in Google as well), check out my book *How to create a YouTube money machine*, inside I give you a detailed run through of my *automated template system* for producing hundreds of promotional videos a day *plus you even get a free two part 30 minute video tutorial as part of the book.*

So few people use this amazing technique that getting yourself ranked on the top page of Google for most keywords is practically a competition free walk in the park! – Word to the wise: GET ON THIS BEFORE EVERYONE ELSE DOES!

A couple of other really good kindle sources for more alternative promotion ideas are here.

33 Ways to SKYROCKET your KINDLE SALES

63 Ways to DRIVE MORE TRAFFIC to your website

Where to go from here

I remember when I wrote my first book nearly 2 decades ago, I was overwhelmed by the sheer volume of information that I had to organize and collate. It seemed insurmountable! I eventually learned to process all my ideas in smaller chunks, implementing them one at a time, and I began creating *systems* to lessen the workload on the repetitive parts*. The important part was I followed the advice of Winston Churchill, and I never, ever gave up!

In fact much of my early frustrations with writing lead to many of the systems and shortcuts you have just learned in this book.

"The journey of a thousand miles begins the first step" as the famous saying goes. I will be the first to tell you that there's no right or wrong way to get started, but the most important thing you *can do* is to actually do it! Start at the beginning of this book and work your way through each of the ideas I've laid out for you. Put them to use and test the results (Progress! - That's the only *true* thing that matters).

As an author you should spend each day taking another step and building another skill - be it writing, promoting or making connections with others that will serve you later. I've been at this since 1992 and when I look back at all I have learned and accomplished since then I'm blown away by how much I've learned and managed to do with my daily addition of knowledge!

Now is the time to take that first step. Outline that first book using the layout techniques I've taught you and then bring it into existence by tomorrow night!

Here's to your future publishing empire!

Dan
:)

2ND·EMPIRE·MEDIA

See more recent titles from us

Power Profits!

Power Profits! Cash Flow Revolution

**63 Ways to DRIVE MORE TRAFFIC
to your website**

**101 TOTALLY FREE ways to market your
website or blog**

How To Build a YouTube Money Machine

The 10 Principles of ENDLESS WEALTH

For our full catalog visit us at:
Wiki-Books.Com